# Wicca For Beginners: Part 1,

*An Introduction to Wiccan Beliefs*

# Table of Contents

Introduction .................................................................................................. 1
**Chapter One: What Is Wicca?** ................................................................. 2
   Origins of Wicca ..................................................................................... 3
   What Wicca Is ......................................................................................... 5
   What Wicca Is Not ................................................................................... 7
   Altar and Tools ........................................................................................ 9
      *Athame* ............................................................................................ 11
      *Cauldron* ......................................................................................... 12
      *Chalice/Goblet* ................................................................................ 13
      *Mortar and Pestle* ........................................................................... 14
      *Wand* .............................................................................................. 15
      *Besom/Broom* ................................................................................ 16
      *Grimoire/Book of Shadows* ............................................................. 17
   Ritual ..................................................................................................... 18
**Chapter Two: What Is Magic?** ............................................................... 21
   Candle Magic ........................................................................................ 24
   Knot Magic ............................................................................................ 25
   Charms and Sachets ............................................................................. 27
      *Talismans and Amulets* .................................................................. 28
   Herb Magic ........................................................................................... 29
   Divination ............................................................................................. 31
   Manifestation ........................................................................................ 33
   Dancing/Movement and Chanting/Singing ........................................... 35
   Sigils ..................................................................................................... 36
**Chapter Three: What Are Spells?** .......................................................... 38
   How to Cast Spells ................................................................................ 42
   Spellcrafting .......................................................................................... 46
      *Spell to Attract Money* .................................................................... 49
**Chapter Four: Spells for Friendship** ...................................................... 51

*Blessing a Friend* ............................................................................................... *53*
*Attracting a New Friend* ................................................................................ *55*
*Hearing From a Friend You Miss* ................................................................. *56*
*Friendship Knot* ............................................................................................. *58*
*Dream Pet Spell* .............................................................................................. *59*
*Repair a Friendship* ....................................................................................... *61*
*Spell for Everlasting Friendship* ................................................................... *62*
*Protection for a Friend* .................................................................................. *64*
*Finding Forgiveness* ....................................................................................... *65*
*Peacefully End a Friendship* ......................................................................... *67*
*Friendship Potion (Drinkable)* ...................................................................... *68*
*Find an Animal Totem or Guide* ................................................................... *70*
*Strengthen a Friendship* ................................................................................ *71*
*Finding a True Friend* .................................................................................... *73*
*Friendship Bag* ................................................................................................ *74*

# Introduction

Congratulations on your purchase of the book *Wicca for Beginners*, and thank you for doing so.

This book will contain plenty of information on the history of Wicca and how it has evolved over the years. The following chapters will cover magic and spells with details on what they are and how to use them. You'll learn some starter spells in popular categories such as friendship, romance, and prosperity.

Not only will you learn about spells and how to cast them, but you'll also learn about the common tools used in Wicca and how they are used in spells and rituals.

After reading this book, you should have the information and knowledge you need to get started on your Wiccan path. You'll have a preliminary guide on the tools and equipment that you should procure to set up your altar and ritual space and have plenty of new spells to try out!

Hopefully, you will have fun getting your feet wet in this new Wiccan venture. This is a Beginner's Guide, and you are always encouraged to keep reading and expanding your studies. However, this is a great place to start! So, go ahead and turn to the next page.

Wicca is a popular topic, and there are so many books out there on the subject. Thank you for choosing to go with this one! Every effort was made to make sure this book is packed full of useful and fun information for you. We hope you enjoy it!

# Chapter One: What Is Wicca?

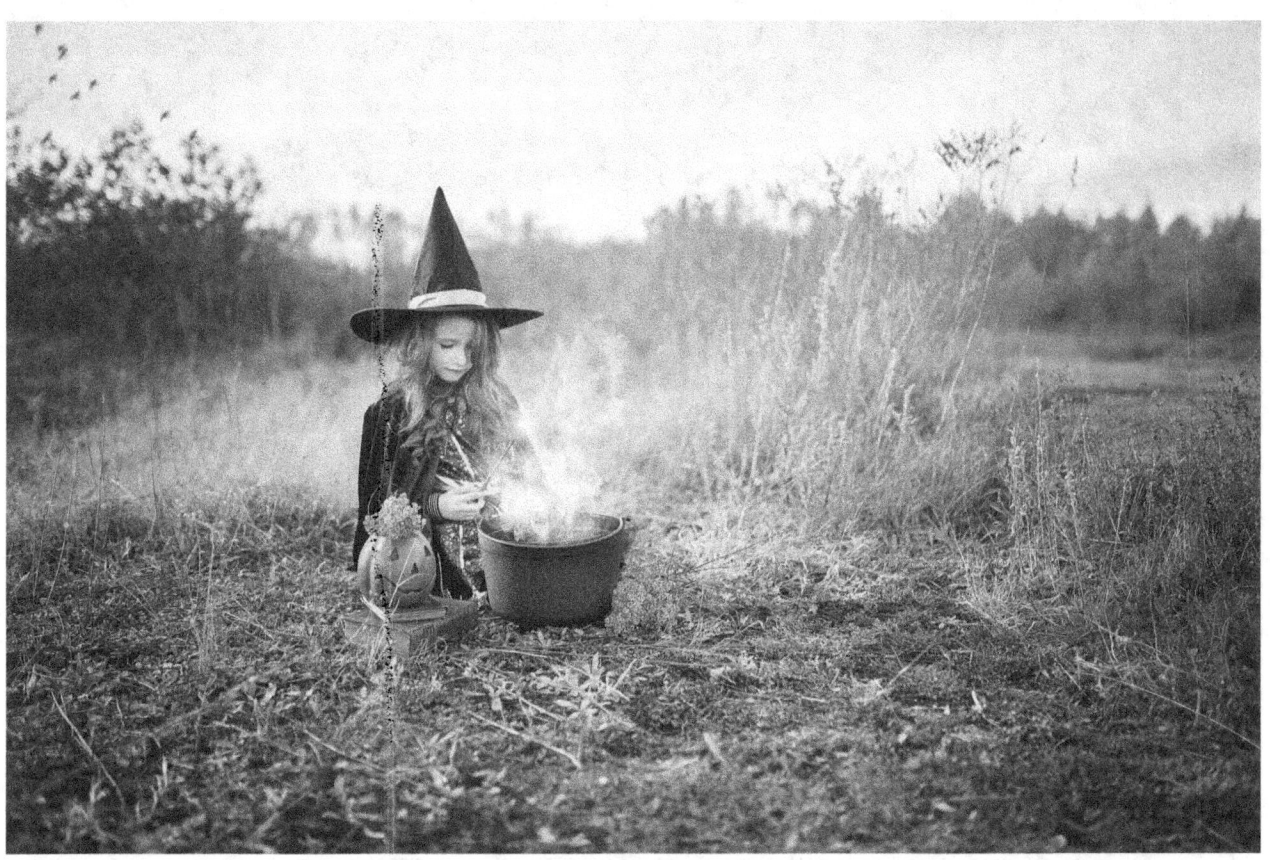

It is time for you to take the first steps on your path as a newly practicing Wiccan. Here is your starting point. Whether you are ready to embrace the Wiccan lifestyle fully or you are interested in learning more about the craft before diving in, this is where you want to start!

You must have questions, like what is Wicca? What are the spells? What is magic? All of these questions will be answered. Take a look at the origins of Wicca to begin your journey.

# Origins of Wicca

Wicca is best described as a modern-day religion that draws on the traditions of ancient witchcraft. While Witchcraft traditions still exist, they are different from Wicca. One can be a Wiccan without being a Witch. Contrary to what media and many other religions would have you believe, Wicca is not evil or destructive. Wicca is a harmonious religion that practices a peaceful and balanced way of life.

Although the ancient traditions have been obscured, rewritten, and removed from history, mainly during the medieval era, it is still possible to glean how those traditions were practiced and then modernize them. Through archeological discovery, the traditions of ancient witchcraft have been understood better.

A main concept of Wicca is pursuing and promoting oneness with the divine and everything that exists. Archaeologists and historians have found ample evidence to show that the original Witchcraft traditions worshipped a Fertility Goddess and a Hunter God. Cave painting evidence suggests that these traditions had been practice for at least 30,000 years. Many of the cave paintings also depict a group of people, such as a coven.

Wicca and Witch are words that derive from the Old English *Wicce*, which referred to a 'Wise Woman' or Healer. Essentially, the origin of Wiccans were women in a community who had knowledge of herbs and plants and used them as medicine and charms. A lot of these practitioners are also referred to as Shamans or Witch Doctors in other cultures.

Gerald Gardner and Doreen Valiente are often attributed with the founding of modern-day Wicca in the early to mid-1900s. Some of the inspiration came from familial traditions that were passed down from generations. Others came from known pre-Christian 'pagan' practices drawn from Ireland, Wales, and Scotland.

Gardner immersed himself in the British Occult during the 1950s and then began to develop a modernized belief system that centered on unity and worship of nature. Magic and spells, as well as the primary worship of a Fertility Goddess and worship of additional deities, such as the Horned God.

After developing his first Coven, Gardner, together with Valiente, worked with the other coven members to structure and write books on this new interpretation of Wicca.

By the 1960s, Wicca had spread to the United States. There was an emphasis on nature, unconventional lifestyles, and a pursuit for the divine and spirituality. Wiccan Covens began to form, usually with 11 to 15 members. Covens usually had a hierarchy of priests and priestesses and included their own structure. Covens encompassed the overall principles of Wicca but allowed the members to build their own traditions and gave them the freedom to include other aspects into their traditions.

Traditional Wicca or Gardnerian Wicca has branched out into many other traditions, such as Norse Wicca, Celtic Wicca, Druidism, Herbal Wicca, Faery Wicca, Eclectic Wicca, and Solitary Wicca.

A few of the common pillars of Wicca include the creed 'An' Harm None, do As you Will.' What this means is that as long as your actions do not intentionally or unintentionally harm someone else, you are free to do what you want. This includes daily activities, tasks, and even magic and spells!

Another important rule that falls into many of the Wiccan traditions is the Law of Three. This law dictates that whatever you put out into the universe is returned to you threefold. This includes positive and negative feelings, thoughts, and actions.

These two main principles outline how Wicca is more about personal growth, spirituality, striving for a better life, and making positive changes in the world.

While each tradition has its own practices and teachings, most traditions follow a typical or similar archetype that is the core of Wicca.

# What Wicca Is

Wicca is both a lifestyle and a belief system. The Path of Wicca encourages practitioners to pursue spirituality, learn about the earth, and find a deeper understanding of the universe and deity. Wicca promotes free-thinking, individuality, and a deep connection to nature. The concept that every living thing is connected to the divine is prevalent in Wicca.

One of the most important lessons that Wicca teaches is responsibility. Wiccans accept responsibility for their actions as one of the important foundations of Wicca, rather than seeking an outside source or an entity of some kind as the cause of temptation or bad behavior. If a Wiccan messes up or does something that harms someone else, then the consequences fall on the Wiccan themselves, no one else.

More than that, Wicca is a celebration of the natural cycles of the planet—the seasons. It celebrates the lunar phases and implements the natural powers of nature, the world, and the universe to cast spells.

Wiccans work with their deities, not in servitude of them. They strive for a life of harmony, peace, and balance. Wiccan spells involve healing, prosperity, harmony, wisdom, creativity, friendship, and romance. Using the power of plants and trees, crystals and rocks, even animals, and the natural elements are how Wiccans harness magic, create spells, and direct their power.

The Goddess and God exist within everyone and everything. Wiccans believe that The Divine can be found in everything, from the smallest flower to the tallest tree. From the crawling ant to the largest whale. The Divine exists in rivers, ocean, clouds, rain, soil, and the air we breathe.

Magic is created from this divine energy. All creations come from combining the elements of earth, air, fire, and water. The sun, moon, and environment become teachers to Wiccans. Providing wisdom and knowledge that has been accumulated throughout the ages, accessing that magic is the source of Wiccan power. This belief creates profound and deep respect for the environment and nature, as well as all life forms.

Wiccans and witches have been persecuted for hundreds of years for their beliefs and practices. This history has created general secrecy regarding Wicca and its traditions. Secrecy isn't required unless it is a specific Coven rule. However, this violent history has also fostered a belief in religious freedom among the Wiccan community. The idea that Wiccan beliefs are not the only beliefs is powerful among Wiccans.

Religious freedom is a strong staple in Wiccan beliefs. Wicca is not the kind of religion that creates missionaries that travel to places to convert new members, growing their numbers and spreading their word. However, Wicca does not turn away those seeking knowledge and answers and those who have an interest in learning.

Overall, Wicca is balanced, peaceful, nature-oriented, and accepting. It is both a religion and a lifestyle that can be pursued by walking many paths, connecting one to the spirit and the divine that exist within everything on this earth.

What Wicca is can't be entirely summed up in a few words or even a few pages! Living the Wiccan lifestyle can be complicated, and it takes practice to understand and embrace the idea fully. It can be a hugely rewarding, empowering, and enlightening path to walk, however. Anyone who is interested is encouraged to learn what they can, find a teacher or a coven, and continue to take this amazing journey for themselves.

# What Wicca Is Not

There are many stigmas surrounding Witchcraft and Wicca regarding what it is and what it isn't. Many of these negative stereotypes have been fueled by the media and entertainment industry. Horror movies and television shows with witches who worship the devil and cast hexes on their enemies have been circulating for years.

Prior to that, Witches and Wiccans were persecuted for their religious beliefs for centuries, primarily by the Catholic Church. Wiccans were said to worship Satan, sell their souls to the devil, and use the devil's power to cast magic and seduce people to their communities to follow Satan.

Unfortunately, there is one major flaw in this logic. The Devil or Satan is a Christian religious entity, not Wiccan.

For thousands of years before Catholicism and Christianity, Wiccans and Witches practiced their beliefs and provided their communities with healing and a connection to nature and the divine. They have never worshipped or believed in an evil entity, and that has been proven through the archeological study of cave paintings.

Now, since Wiccans don't believe in an entity such as the devil, how can they worship him? Well, the easy answer is they can't.

The Hunter God has often been depicted in cave paintings as a man wearing Stag antlers, or as a man with a stag head. These portrayals of the Hunter God are a representation of his masculinity and his connection to the forest and the animals. Many ancient religious rituals and practices involve the wearing of animal skins or animal parts, such as feathers in Native American headdresses, or furs that are worn by Shamans and Witch Doctors.

It could very well be a coincidence that Christianity developed an evil goat-like entity (similar to a stag) that symbolizes temptation, destruction, and evil. However, there is some evidence to suggest that such an entity was created in an attempt to convert people and communities away from Wicca and Witchcraft.

Please keep in mind that Wicca is not devil worship; it has never been about devil worship. If other religions have evil entities that are part of their theology, that isn't bad or wrong. Wicca, however, does not subscribe to such beliefs.

On a larger scale, Wiccans believe in doing the right thing because it is the right thing. They do not believe in an evil entity that threatens eternal damnation to keep them from behaving badly. Some people may need more structure and that firm guiding hand to remind them how they should live their lives.

Wicca is not a cult. Covens do not gather under a single, supreme leader that seeks to spread their word, recruit more members, and convert others to their faith. There is no extremism in Wicca, as Wicca is a very balanced, peaceful belief system.

Magic and spiritual power are drawn from the four elements, from nature, and from the universe. Wiccans do not steal power or the life force of other people or animals to cast their spells. Magic is a pure form of energy that is not manipulative or sourced by stealing life and strength from others.

On the subject of spells and magic, Wiccans do not use spells to cast hexes on others. They do not seek to control the hearts and minds of anyone else, and they do not destroy or disrupt the lives of others. Remember that first Law, 'An Harm None, Do as You Will?' That extends to spells and magic, too. That 'none' doesn't just apply to people, either. All life is included in that concept.

Of course, Wiccans aren't perfect. No one is, really. As humans, we can't always abstain from negative thoughts and feelings. Sometimes, we blame others and think we are the victims. The same flaws that exist in humans exist in Wiccans, as well.

While Wiccans believe that the Law of Three will correct any imbalances in thoughts and behavior, it is also important to make a conscious effort before performing a ritual or casting a spell. Sometimes, spells designed for the best intentions may end up having unwanted consequences. Wiccans try to carefully consider outcomes that could potentially affect others and how they will be affected.

There are many things Wicca isn't. If you have any concerns, keep reading, and decide for yourself. There are also communities you can join to get your questions answered if this book doesn't give you what you need. As always, you are encouraged to find answers and seek knowledge.

## Altar and Tools

The Wiccan Altar is an important aspect of Wiccan practices. The altar is usually a stationary location that is used for casting spells, rituals, even meditations, and other Wiccan practices.

While your altar doesn't have to be stationary, many practitioners find it beneficial to have a designated location for practicing and casting magic. Magic and spells can be cast anywhere at any time. Many rituals are performed outside; some spells are cast in specific rooms of the house. A temporary altar can be set up for these occasions, or the ritual can be performed without an altar under these circumstances.

Every Wiccan's altar is going to be different. Some practitioners use a coffee table or bedside table with just a few candles. Others have a specially crafted table that has carved designs or a special tapestry on them. Some altars don't even have a table but are just a designated spot on the floor with a tapestry or blanket. When you begin to set up your own altar, do what feels right for you. The most decorative or expensive altar might look great, but if it doesn't flow with your energy or wishes in an altar, stick to what makes sense for you.

An altar can be as decorated or bare as you would like. There are some common tools that are often found on a Wiccan altar, though, and some are not such common tools.

Some basic altar designs or setups include having a candle at each of the four cardinal directions—north, east, south, and west—and objects to represent each of the four elements—earth, air, fire, and water. This includes a candle to represent both the Goddess and the God and objects to represent other deities, as well. Generally, there should be an incense burner since it is very commonly used in rituals and spells.

The more common tools usually found on a Wiccan's altar include the following:

- Athame
- Cauldron
- Chalice or goblet
- Mortar and pestle
- Wand
- Besom or Broom
- Grimoire or Book of Shadows

Now, if you decide to join a Coven, there is usually a central altar where your Coven gathers and a single Grimoire or Book of Shadows that the Coven defaults to. Every

Coven is going to be different. Whether or not individuals have their own altars or Grimoire is going to be specific to the Coven you joined.

## *Athame*

An Athame is a black-handled, double-edged ritual knife. It is associated with the element of fire and masculine energy. Often, the Athame isn't even a sharpened blade, as it has more of a ritual symbolism than a tool used for cutting and slicing.

Athames are commonly used for carving symbols in candle wax, dirt, or sand. They can also be used to channel energy and lay down energetic barriers. Since the Athame is associated with fire, it can be set on your altar as the object that represents this element.

## *Cauldron*

Cauldrons are commonly depicted in media and art as a large cast-iron pot over a fire with a boiling, goopy brew with several cloaked witches standing around it, mixing the potion. Cauldrons, however, have many, many uses.

Cauldrons come in many shapes and sizes. Some are only two inches across, while others can be thirteen inches across or large enough to cook an entire soup over an open fire. Some are bowl-shaped, and others are potbellied. Some cauldrons have lids and handles, while others don't. You might find a cauldron with feet, while others sit on a flat bottom.

Most cauldrons are cast-iron or metal that is painted black. They can be used for many parts of a Wiccan ritual. Cauldrons make effective incense holders. They can also be a container for fire during fire rituals, as long as they are fire-safe metal or material. Cauldrons can be used to mix ingredients together, and if they are food-safe, they can be used to make brews, infusions, and other ingestible magical mixtures.

Whenever you mix ingredients that are meant to be consumed or used directly on the skin, make sure that the cauldron or other equipment that you are using has been labeled food-safe and heat-safe. Many cauldrons on the market today are painted black or not made of pure cast iron, and they can leak toxicity into the food being cooked.

## *Chalice/Goblet*

A chalice or goblet is another versatile tool. They can be fancy and made of expensive metal and decorated with engravings and jewels, or it could be a simple carved wooden cup.

The chalice represents the element of water. It can be used in rituals for drinking libations and honoring the Goddess and God. Additionally, the chalice is associated with springtime but also the Magic Well. Many Celtic myths and legends include a reference to a Magic Well that can be the source of great power or used in divination (which will be covered more in a later chapter).

## *Mortar and Pestle*

A mortar and pestle is a combination tool. It generally comes with a bowl-shaped base and a wide and broad grinding tool. The mortar and pestle can be placed on the altar or just easily accessible for spells and rituals.

A mortar and pestle are used to grind herbs, resins, seeds, and other plant materials that are used in magic. Whether it is to make a spell powder, your own incense, or a charm bag, a mortar and pestle are important in crafting herb magic.

Having a separate mortar and pestle strictly for food use and then one for ritual use is often recommended. There are many ways to incorporate magic in cooking and in the kitchen. If you have any interest in learning about food and cooking magic, having a mortar and pestle only for food is a good idea.

## *Wand*

Wands are not an essential tool when it comes to Wicca. They also carry media stigmas, such as in the popular movie series *Harry Potter*, where wands are used by witches and wizards to cast spells.

A wand is a masculine object associated with the element air. Wands are versatile; they can be made of metal, wood, or any material, really. Some are hollow and filled with herbs and crystals; others might have runes carved on them or are more intricate and decorative.

Wands are used in channeling and directing magical power. They are not a key component in spellcasting or ritual. However, they can be instrumental when creating sigils for spells (sigils will be covered in greater detail in later chapters). When casting your Sacred Circle, the wand can help lay down a protective, energetic barrier.

## *Besom/Broom*

Have you ever seen a movie with witches flying around on broomsticks? Or maybe you've seen a Halloween decoration of a witch on a broom in front of a full moon? Witches on brooms have served as popular decorations for Halloween and related holidays.

Did you know that brooms are actually used in Wicca? While you probably won't be taking any midnight flights on your own broomstick, brooms do have a symbolic meaning and use in ritual and Wicca.

The ritual broom is referred to as a Besom. They are commonly used in magic and spells meant for clearing away negative energies and cleansing a space or a room. The act of sweeping can be symbolic or real when using a Besom in ritual.

There are some beautifully crafted besoms on the market with feathers, ribbons, and fancy colors. However, like with all the ritual tools, choose the one that you resonate with most. Fancy and expensive brooms do not necessarily mean better. Magical tools are driven by their wielder's intention, not how they look or what they are decorated with.

## *Grimoire/Book of Shadows*

Another term that has some media stereotypes is the Wiccan Book of Shadows. Covens usually keep a central Book of Shadows for all of their teachings. However, keeping your own isn't a bad idea. If you are a solitary practitioner, you definitely want to keep a Book of Shadows.

During the years of persecution, having a Book of Shadows could lead to a death sentence, which is why, sometimes, they were written in code. Some Covens still carry on that tradition, so the code may only be known to the High Priestess or High Priest of the Coven.

A Grimoire or Book of Shadows is a culmination of the information and knowledge you have gathered as a Wiccan. It also serves as a journal of your spiritual journey. These books tend to hold rituals, spells, and information on deities, histories of the Coven, or practitioner. You can also write down your thoughts, feelings, and experiences when performing rituals or spells in your Book of Shadows.

Some practitioners will write in their Book of Shadows every day. There is no right or wrong way to keep a Book of Shadows. If you are more artistically inclined, you might like to draw pictures and images to corresponding topics in your Book of Shadows. You may also like to print out pictures for the same effect. Or, you might only put written words in your Book of Shadows.

The book becomes a sacred text as you write it. Not only does it contain your spiritual and magical experiences, but it also contains your own practices and beliefs or your Coven's.

Many Wiccans like to make their own tools if they can. It can be very empowering, and they connect you with all the tools in your craft.

## Ritual

While not all Wiccan traditions follow the same paths and principles, a common element in all traditions is a Ritual. Wiccan Ritual is at the core of many Wiccan practices. Whether it is to celebrate a lunar phase like New Moon or Full Moon, holidays such as the Esbats and Sabbats, or important milestones like handfasting (weddings), initiations, or life celebration ceremonies, a Ritual is performed in various forms for each.

If you belong to a Coven, then more often than not, your Coven will gather to perform such rituals together. However, if you are a solitary practitioner, performing rituals on your own is also important.

A ritual tends to be an event to honor the Goddess and God and celebrate the universe and how it works—the changing of the seasons or lunar phases, giving thanks for the harvest, or making it through the winter.

Generally, no two Wiccan Rituals are the same. Covens tend to hold highly structured and elaborate rituals. On the flip side, sometimes, solitary practitioners will make up a ritual as they go along, rather than have a predetermined notion or choreography to follow.

The content of each ritual will vary based on what the ritual is for. A Full Moon ritual will be focused on The Goddess and honoring her. There are holiday celebrations that honor springtime and new beginnings or solstices. Some rituals will focus on the relationship between the Goddess and God and may venture into a more sexual nature.

While rituals vary from Coven to Coven, practitioner to practitioner, and tradition to tradition, there are some basic components to each ritual.

The elements of ritual include:

- Purification of participants and space
- Setting the Altar
- Casting the Sacred Circle
- Invocations
- Intention is Set
- Heart of Ritual is performed
- Thanking Deity
- Closing Sacred Circle

Purification for the practitioner or participants in the ritual can be in the form of a ritual bath or with smudging or another preferred method of purification. The space where the ritual is held should be purified as well.

Next, the altar should be set, often at the center of where the sacred circle is being cast. Casting the circle can be a type of ritual in itself, especially in a Coven, and it creates a barrier between the practitioners and the rest of the world. During the invocations, this is generally when the Goddess and God are invited to join the ritual, as well as the elements earth, air, fire, and water.

Once invocations are complete, an intention for the ritual should be set. This intention should be in line with the goal of the ritual. If it is an initiation ritual, the intention could be that all new initiates are fully welcomed into the circle. If it is a harvest ritual, the intention could be as simple as to give thanks for the bountiful harvest.

The heart of the ritual is where many different tasks can be performed for honoring. Sometimes, covens will put on a dramatic scene. A solitary practitioner might write a poem and read it aloud. There can be a time for spellcasting, meditation, divination, and other magical practices that enhance rituals, as well. Many rituals include dancing, chanting, or drumming of some kind.

Many rituals will designate a time for cakes and wine, which is a kind of ritual feasting where portions of the food and drink are offered to the Goddess and God.

Once the tasks of the ritual are complete, it is always important to thank your deities and properly close your sacred circle. You may find that you need to ground yourself after a ritual. This is common.

Rituals are quite subjective, and as you practice, you will get a feel for performing tasks that are oriented toward your ritual's intention. Stick to what feels right for you, and you'll begin to develop your own methods for rituals.

# Chapter Two: What Is Magic?

The word magic has had many meanings and uses throughout history. Commonly, magic refers to using tricks and illusions to portray magical events. Performers have used these illusions for hundreds of years as a form of entertainment.

Some popular illusions include pulling a rabbit out of a hat and escape artists freeing themselves from potentially deadly and impossible situations. Magic with clown cars, where a bunch of clowns emerges from a tiny car, is a type of illusion magic, as well as the magic where the person who manages to get your watch off your wrist while talking to you, without you noticing!

This kind of magic is purely for entertainment value.

For Wiccans, magic isn't an entertainment platform. Magic is a skill and tool that is used as part of the Wiccan lifestyle. In terms of Wicca and Witchcraft, the word magic is defined as the art of intentionally directing the co-creative forces of the universe by directing natural and universal energy to effect desired changes.

Everything is made up of energy. Modern-day science has the equipment to measure energy in the form of heatwaves, sound waves, light waves, and several other forms. These types of equipment can measure the energy fields in and around any kind of object. Electrical currents exist within all living creatures, including humans. The earth itself has a molten lava core that is composed of heat and light energy.

Wiccans have spent thousands of years studying these energies, learning about how each type of energy has power and how it can be used to make changes. A change can be as small as healing a headache or having softer skin, or as complex as calling a rainstorm or another weather change.

Energies interact with each other naturally. Wiccans can influence and direct those natural energies to interact differently. This is what creates magic.

Generally speaking, Wiccans use magic to improve their lives and circumstances. Magic is frequently used to improve health, prosperity, love, protection, and overall well-being. That doesn't mean that magic can't be used for someone else. It is imperative, however, to get permission from someone else if you plan to cast a spell or use magic on their behalf.

The rule 'An Harm None, Do as You Will' is very important when it comes to magic. Magic can be used with the best of intentions, but if you cast a spell for someone without their permission, you could be forcing them to deal with something they aren't ready to face or pushing them out of their comfort zone without their consent. This is frowned upon.

Additionally, using magic to get your way with someone, such as a love spell cast on a specific person, is again forcing your will on someone else, and that is not appropriate. Magic isn't meant to control someone else, hurt other people, or disrupt the balance of their lives. You'll just need their expressed permission if you want to use magic for their sake.

Intention and magical goals are two important components when making magic. Regardless of your method or tradition, intention and goal are both keys to making successful magic. Before you begin casting magic, set your intention, and know your goal. This will help ensure success.

Magic today is varied. Depending on the tradition you follow, you may only learn about certain types of magic. You may only have a personal interest in one type and never expand beyond that. Most Wiccans lean toward natural elements and tools when creating magic. Sometimes, no tools are needed at all, such as when you decide to create magic through dancing and chanting.

Types of Magic:

- Candle Magic
- Cord Magic
- Charms and Sachets
- Talismans and Amulets
- Herb Magic
- Divination
- Manifestation
- Dancing/Movement and Chanting/singing
- Sigils

You'll discover your preferred forms of magic. You may want to dabble in a few different types to get a better understanding of magic as a whole. Don't be afraid to keep studying and learning more about magic and the various ways to use magic!

Most of the more commonly used magical methods are based on some folklore or older traditions from Celtic Lore and other ancient civilizations. These were some of the first practices of Wiccans from early civilizations. However, some methods are drawn from older Occult sources, specifically more ceremonial magic.

# Candle Magic

Candle magic is pretty self-explanatory. Magic can be created through the burning of a candle. If you set your intention and goal and burn a candle while focusing on and visualizing that intention and goal, that intention is released into the universe, as the candle burns.

Candle magic can be enhanced by anointing the candle with essential or herbal oils. You can carve runes or symbols into the candle wax to increase the potency of the magic. Also, selecting a candle that has a color appropriate to your intention and goal is another way to enhance the magic in candles.

Candle magic can be very basic and only include one candle. Sometimes, when casting specific spells with candles, you might need more than one, and a spell can sometimes call for candles of a specific color.

Not all magic has to be ceremonial and ritualistic. Candle magic is a great example of how simple some magic can be! The simplicity of a spell doesn't reduce its effectiveness, however.

Before using a candle in a spell, it is a good idea to cleanse the candle. You can do this by passing it through the smoke of burning incense or submerging it in a dish of sea salt.

Usually, when using candle magic, you'll want to burn the candle for three consecutive nights while it is sitting on your altar. You can repeat your intention or goal while it burns, or visualize your goal. Including chanting and music is another great way to add magical potency to your spell.

Once the three nights are complete, keep the remaining candle stub in a magical place, or bury it in the ground.

## Knot Magic

Knot magic is a form of magic that is primarily designed to store magical power and intention and then release it over a period of time.

To start, you'll want a 9-inch piece of string or cord. You can use a 9-foot cord, as well, if you are not planning on storing your cord in a small space. You can keep magic stored in the knots for as long as you need and then release them at a more appropriate time.

For a typical knot magic spell, you are going to be tying 9 knots. Start on the left end, then the right end. The third knot will be tied in the middle of the cord. You'll then keep tying the new knot between the two most recently tied while alternating from the left side to the right side.

As you tie each knot visualize your goal and say the following chant for each knot.

*By knot 1, the spell has begun*
*By knot 2, it cometh true*
*By knot 3, so mote it be*
*By knot 4, magic power I store*
*By knot 5, this spell's alive*
*By knot 6, this spell I fix*
*By knot 7, my goal I'll leaven*
*By knot 8, this will be fate*
*By knot 9, what's done is mine*

Once each knot has been tied, your power is stored. The knots should be tied in one ritual, but they can only be released one knot a day once you start. They should be released in the same order in which they are tied. Untie your knots over nine consecutive days to release the stored magic into the universe toward your goals.

Before untying a knot, hold the cord in your hand and re-visualize your goal. Speak it aloud if that will help, and untie the knot to release the magic.

Knots don't just have to be used in this standard knot ritual. Magical knots are also used in handfasting ceremonies and joining spells and magic. Knots can hold power, combine energies, and bind energies together.

# Charms and Sachets

Charms and sachets can essentially be the same thing. Generally, a charm or sachet is a bag of cloth or a pouch that has been filled with herbs or other magical catalysts, such as crystals or personal power items. These bags or pouches can be carried on a person or placed in a specific area for the magic to spread.

Some Wiccans will purchase premade pouches, while others prefer to make their own out of cloth and string. The color of the pouch can improve the spell potency, as can the type and color of yarn or string used to bind the sachet.

When making a sachet or charm bag, you'll want to lay the pouch and add your magical ingredients to the pouch. Sometimes, there is an incantation to go along with the assembly of your charm bag. Other times, there is an order in which your ingredients should be added. While making your charm bag, visualization of your intention is important.

You should assemble your charm or sachet on your altar.

Sachets can be carried on your person, in a pocket, purse, or backpack. They can be placed under your pillow, hung in a closet, or set in the glove compartment of your car. Generally, the spell you cast will give specifics about where your sachet should be placed.

Additionally, you should give your charm bag a squeeze periodically to release the magical power. When you do this, remember to visualize your goal and intention. This will continue to enhance the magical power.

## *Talismans and Amulets*

Talismans are manmade objects that are imbued with magical powers. Amulets are natural objects charged with magic and enhanced by their existing natural magical power.

A talisman can be a ring, a pendant, a coin, a figurine, or any object that is manmade, usually small enough to wear or keep in a pocket or bag.

Amulets can be crystals, rocks, a piece of bark, a feather, and objects existing in nature. Since these objects are already connected to their own source of natural magic, sometimes choosing an amulet with associations that align with your intention and goal is a great idea when making magic!

Before charging a talisman or amulet, you'll want to cleanse it by passing it through incense smoke, submerging it in sea salt, or using another preferred cleansing method.

Talismans and amulets are both used to enhance personal power. To charge them with magic, you'll want to set the object on your altar or hold it in your hand while sitting at your altar. Using clear visualization, create your magical intention and goal.

You can anoint talismans and amulets with essential or herbal oils to increase magical potency. You can sing or chant or play music over them or while holding them to increase the magical power.

Once fully charged, you'll want to keep your talisman or amulet on your person for three days, then keep it in a magical place. While wearing it, periodically touch your talisman or amulet, and when you do, clearly visualize your magical goal.

Charged objects are incredibly powerful. Once charged, that object is going to be aligned with a specific goal or intention. When you carry it on you, that charged energy will mix with your own energy to enforce the desired outcome.

You may have seen some jewelers selling charged pendants or rings. Any charged object can be powerful. However, talismans and amulets that you charge yourself are going to work the best for your own goals and desires.

## Herb Magic

Herbal magic is again pretty self-explanatory. Magic and spells that are cast with the use of fresh plants, flowers, or plant parts, as well as dried herbs, flowers, and plant parts. Even herbal oils and essential oils qualify as herb magic.

Herb magic has a wide variety of uses. Making and burning herbal incense is a form of herb magic. Cooking with magical herbs makes a meal magical. Soaking in an herb bath adds magic to regular bathing.

Plants, flowers, trees, and herbs all contain powerful magic. They grow out of the earth and receive nutrients from the sun and water, and they breathe our air. Plants are a great combination of the four natural elements and their associated powers.

Most herbs have both medicinal and magical properties. Learning to utilize both magic and medicine is a great use of a Wiccan's power and talent. Natural medicine is incredibly potent and has significantly fewer side effects than more conventional medicines.

Some common types of herb magic include:

- Incense burning
- Herbal charm bags
- Magical cooking
- Herbal baths
- Herbals teas
- Herbal body products and cosmetics

If you use soap, lotion, shampoo, perfume, or other hygiene and cosmetic items, making your own with essential oils or dried herbs is a great way to benefit from herbal magic. Any time you craft something with herbs, you'll want to visualize the desired goal while making that item. When soaking in an herb bath, visualization of your intention is key, as well as when you cook an herbal meal, burn incense, and drink herbal tea.

The magical and medicinal properties of the individual herbs greatly enhance spells and magic. However, intent and desire are still important to the direction and creation of magic.

Herbs can easily be combined to make powders and placed in sachets and charms. An herbal powder constructed from the right herbs can be sprinkled in doorways for protection of the home.

Burning incense in a new home or smudging with an herb bundle can cast out negative or unwanted energies.

Natural ingredients, such as plants and herbs, are so potent in magical power. You can grow and harvest your own herbs, as many Wiccans geared toward herbal magic like doing. Most herbs and plant pieces can be harvested without killing the plant as well.

If you do harvest your own herbs and plants, it is important to remember to ask permission from the plant, give thanks, and also leave a gift to the plant and Earth Goddess. This goes any time you take something out of nature, including amulets. When you take something, you always have to give something back. This is a balance, and this is how you show your appreciation to the deity.

## Divination

If you've ever seen a movie with a Gypsy, Shaman, or Witch casting runes, bones, or using tarot cards, then you've seen some commercial interpretations of divination.

Divination is a type of magic in which the Wiccan practitioner is seeking answers or direction. They use a catalyst to raise magical energy in order to receive guidance. Divination does require the practitioner to enter a light meditative state and to focus and visualize their question or concern strongly.

Divination isn't just about finding answers, though. Sometimes, it is about finding clarity or discerning the proper path or direction or action to take.

Common forms of divination include:

- Tarot Cards
- Runes
- Scrying (crystal ball, a bowl of water, black mirror, fire)
- Ouija Board/Witch Board
- Dousing (pendulum, dousing or divining rods)

There are many different kinds of tarot cards. Some are more traditional with the major and minor arcana, and others are more specialized to angels or Shamans. There are many ways to use Tarot cards for divining. You can do complex card spreads for yourself, or just draw a single card every day. Many Wiccans who practice Tarot will draw a card every morning to help set the tone of their day.

Rune sets are usually based on the Nordic Runes of the Vikings. Like Tarot cards, runes can be spread in a specific layout for guidance. They can also be cast or scattered out on your altar for a more randomized spread.

Scrying is a form of divination where the practitioner enters a light meditative state and stares into a catalyst, such as a crystal ball, and receives information, often in the form of images that can then be interpreted as answers.

The Ouija Board or Witch Board is most commonly seen as a children's board game now, but that doesn't mean there isn't power in it. Ouija boards can communicate with many different entities, including spirits, angels, and darker entities. Without the proper intention and protections set, they can potentially let negative energies and entities into your space. However, if used correctly, there is a lot to be learned from the spirits that can be contacted.

Dousing is the process of using a pendulum or dowsing rods to follow energetic currents. If you ask a pendulum a question, it'll swing in one direction for 'yes' and another direction for 'no.' Several Wiccans carry pendulums with them and pull it out of their pocket or purse to answer daily questions for themselves.

Whenever you use divination, there should be an overall intention or goal to receive the information that serves your highest good. Some forms of divination require more in-depth study or practice with meditation to master.

In most cases, the information you receive from divination will need to be translated. If you ever do divination reading for yourself, write down everything you see, feel, learn, or read. At first glance, it might not make sense. Then think about your question or goal and play around with what you have written until it starts to makes sense.

When pursuing divination, it is important to remember that nothing is set. Any action, no matter how small, can alter the course that you are on. If you use divination to answer a question for yourself, the answer you receive is only relevant if you stay on the exact path you are on at the time you ask the question.

That said, how can you ever really learn anything from divination? Well, first of all, more than one road leads to the same destination. What that means is that multiple choices might bring you to the same resolution. There isn't ever a single right or wrong way to get to where you want to be or where you are meant to be.

Using divination magic is more of a way to guide yourself or even find out what you need to do to get to where you want to be. Life is always changing.

## Manifestation

The art of manifestation is often something we do every day without even realizing it. However, when combined with magical power, manifestation can become much more potent and effective.

Manifestation is the act of desiring something and willing it into being. For example, if you want to buy a house and you spend a few minutes every day focusing your energy on manifesting the perfect house for your needs and wants, you'll be surprised at how fast you'll come across your heart's desire.

A few keys to proper manifestation include visualizing your goals as if they have already happened. Thinking in terms of 'I am' or 'I have,' rather than 'I want' or 'I will.' Align yourself with wish fulfillment, release your unlimited consciousness, and acknowledge and accept your strong personal power and connection to the divine.

A great time to incorporate manifestation into daily practices is during meditations. Speaking manifestations aloud enforces their power and strength. Phrase them in a way that sounds like it has already come to pass. Write it one on a piece of paper every day and then burn that paper every night to release the magical intention to the universe.

A manifestation is a powerful tool for getting what you want. It isn't an instant process, however. Sometimes, the intent has to be put out into the universe multiple times or repeatedly before the energies start to work for you. Clear and strong visualization is going to make manifesting more powerful.

# Dancing/Movement and Chanting/Singing

As previously touched on, energy exists in heatwaves and sound waves. That energy becomes magic! Moving the body through dance creates heat, and singing, chanting, or even playing a drum or rattle creates sound waves. These are both forms of raising magical power that have been used for thousands of years.

Ancient rituals include drum circles, dancing around bonfires, and chanting invocations and incantations to the Goddess and God. Dancing and music are some of the oldest forms of magical power in human society.

Even before there was human speech or the concept of dance, movement could be used. The ritual of hunting or running through the woods to spear a prey is a very old form of magical power and expression that has been used since the early man. Different instruments like drums, rattles, and dried gourds have been incorporated in ritual and magic for a very long time as well.

Our bodies are full of magical power. Movement and voice belong to us personally and can create an empowered feeling when working magic. Additionally, our own bodies and voices add a touch of personal power to spells and magic that only enhance their effectiveness.

During a spell or ritual, adding a chant or incantation can increase the chances of success of that spell. Dancing around your circle during a spell will also continue to raise that energy and your success. When dancing or chanting, remember to keep visualizing your intention for the magic.

## Sigils

Sigils are a unique form of magic in a way that you can never use the same one twice. There are many methods for drawing and creating your own sigils, but the basic idea is to visualize a goal in the form of a sentence or phrase.

Write that sentence or phrase down on paper. First, cross out any repeating letters. Some Wiccans will take out any vowels, as well. However, you can choose whether you want to leave the vowels or not. Next, you are going to break the remaining letters down to their most basic geometrical shapes.

For example, an H will be broken down into | - | and an O would become ( ). Once you've done this with all the letters, you can combine and rearrange the basic shapes into a pleasing arrangement for yourself.

After you have your sigil as you want it, surround it with a circle, square, or triangle shape.

While creating your sigil, you will want to read your intention aloud and continue to visualize it.

Once the sigil is created, you can use a finger or your wand to draw the sigil on yourself, on objects, and on walls, and continue to visualize. When you draw the sigil, the magical intention is released into whatever it is drawn on.

You can further activate sigils with meditation, crystals, or charging it with personal power.

Once the sigil has been used, dispose of your paper copy. Many Wiccans will burn their sigils once they have been cast. While disposing of them isn't necessary, sigils are designed for single use. They are not designed to linger. Rather, they become part of the universe and work their magical purpose subtly. Once released, their magic is constant.

There are many different ways to make your own sigils, and there is no right or wrong way to create or activate them. Play around with it, and see what works for you.

Magic comes in many forms and has many uses. It can be called forth and directed in so many different ways. You don't always need special tools and ingredients when making magic. Magic can be simple and complex. Different kinds of magic can be combined for more complex spells and increase magical potency.

Please remember that when making magic, even with strong visualization and intention, the magic needs reinforcement from you to keep working. Consider this; if you cast a spell to get a job, but you never search for or apply for any jobs, more than likely, the magical energy will fizzle out.

If you do not continue to reinforce your intention and goal, then your magic many never reach its destination, and the spell becomes unsuccessful. Magic is powerful, and so are you!

# Chapter Three: What Are Spells?

We've talked about what magic is, as well as the different kinds of magic. So then, what is a spell? How does it differ from magic? How do you cast a spell?

These are very good questions!

Spells do not constitute waving a magic wand or saying magical words and having all your wishes and desires granted immediately. Movies and television shows seem to think that is how magic works. The magic that is locked away in every being and object on the planet is much more subtle but still powerful!

Magic is a broader term to describe the energy and the power Wiccans have to direct and change the course of that energy to achieve their goals.

Spells are the catalyst by which Wiccans use magic for their goals and intentions.

Essentially, casting a spell is a Wiccan's ability to perform a magical task that effects energetic change.

Spells are small rituals in a sense. They can be as simple as the burning of a single candle or the singing of a song. They can be more complex with various ingredients, tasks, and incantations.

Spells have been used since the Ancient Egyptian society, as well as ancient Greek, Roman, and Nordic societies. These are some of the earliest known civilizations that used sigils, sacred circles, wands, and magical words.

A few common components of spellcasting include visualizing and stating your intention and goal. It also includes raising magical power in yourself and around you and then releasing that power out toward your desires. Once the spell is cast, reinforcing the magic over the next few days will ensure a greater chance of success with spells.

A basic spell commonly involves an incantation, the implementation of tools or ingredients, and a set of actions. Together, these components direct the spell's intention and energy to effect change properly.

While there isn't necessarily a right or wrong way to perform spells, it is a good idea to have a plan in mind or a written spell to cast before you start. Trying to make them up as you go isn't wrong, but as a beginner, it is a good idea to get used to spellcasting first. Sometimes spells are organized and call for a specific order of events or ingredients.

The magic of spells can also be influenced by outside forces, such as the lunar cycles and seasons. While there are recommended times to cast certain spells, this is not a requirement. If someone needs a healing spell or requests a healing spell, it would be inappropriate to tell them you had to wait three weeks for the moon to be in the proper cycle. The individual might not have that time or want to wait.

That said, let us take a look at lunar cycles and how they can impact spells.

During the waxing moon, when the moon is growing to its full state, it is an ideal time to cast spells for new beginnings, growth, initiations, enhancements, inspiration, freedom, vitality, love, prosperity, friendship, health, and luck. Generally, spells that draw something to you are best cast during the waxing moon.

On the night of the full moon, the best spells to cast include spells for manifesting goals, passion, healing, strength, knowledge, power, love, dreams, legal matters, protection, divination, and finding new employment. Any kind of spell that is strongly goal-oriented or seeking fruition of manifestations can be cast on the full moon.

When the moon is waning, going from the full state to the new state, it is a great time to cast spells to banish evil, remove obstacles, neutralize enemies, remove harm, banish illness, and banish addiction. This is the time to cast spells that banish, remove, or end any unwanted action, behavior, or energy.

At the New Moon, it is a good time to cast spells for new beginnings, new ventures, love, romance, good health, and job hunting. It's a good time to cast spells that involve anything new.

When considering the seasons, springtime is the season for casting spells that have to do with new beginnings, growth, starting over, and overcoming hardships. It's a good time to cast spells for fertility, love, and cleaning out the old.

Summer is a great time to cast spells for weddings or marriage. This is also the time for magic focused on male fertility and energy, as well as legal contracts.

During the fall, spells to harvests, endings, and legal contracts are at their strongest.

Winter is the time to cast spells for family connections, hearth and home, and new beginnings. This is also the time of the Sun God returning from the underworld.

Spells are not designed to be used to manipulate, control, or dominate anyone else. These magics are essentially forbidden and are strongly frowned upon. It goes back to that original law we discussed of 'An Harm None, Do as You Will.' That law is going to continue to surface in your Wiccan studies.

For example, and this is a common one, you have a crush on someone, or you are in love with them, and you want them to love you back. It is commonly thought that casting a love spell directly on someone is the best way to gain their affections. Unfortunately, that isn't the case. Casting a spell that directs someone else's affections to be altered or changed is considered harmful and manipulative.

Here's a scenario. What if you cast that love spell on a specific person, but you realize they smell bad, or you find that you don't really like them, or they become obsessive? Even worse, what if they turn out to be abusive or manipulative or constantly unfaithful? Now you have altered someone's feelings for your own gain, and you won't even want to be in a relationship with them.

This is a very good example of why you should not cast a spell directly on someone else.

An alternative spell to cast is a 'bring love to me' spell (which will be covered in greater detail in the Romance Spells chapter). These spells don't target a specific person but open you up to attracting someone that is good for you and vice versa.

Spells should be geared toward improvement, balance, harmony, peace, and personal growth. Even so, the Law of Three states that any energy someone puts out into the world, positive or negative, will come back threefold. For Wiccans who don't follow the Harm None law, they will receive their own form of energetic backlash.

Generally, when following the Wiccan lifestyle, casting spells for positive change and resolution are more appealing to a Wiccan than anything negative.

So, what are spells? Spells are the ritual that Wiccans use to invoke and direct magical energies and power to create positive changes. Spells should always be cast with the intention of serving the highest of all involved.

While Wiccans primarily cast spells for their own desires and intentions, you can cast spells for others. It is important to have the expressed permission of someone else before casting a spell on their behalf. This is to continue to uphold the Harm None law. Even if you cast spells with the best of intentions but without permission, you are imposing a change on a person without their consent. This can unintentionally cause harm.

Don't be afraid of spells and magic, though. Once you learn to cast spells and access that magic, you may learn more about yourself and your path than you ever thought possible!

Spells are pretty great and can be used for just about anything, as long as no one is being harmed. As you read through the types of spells, you may notice that they pertain to a lot of tasks, actions, and desires. Sometimes, they are so mundane you might be asking yourself, "Is magic even necessary for that?"

The truth is, casting a spell isn't always necessary. However, Wiccans often find empowerment in casting spells. It gives them a deeper sense of control over their own life and fate. It creates a sense of positivity around certain feelings and situations. Spells do not only effect change in the world, but the practitioner also feels the change within themselves.

When your own energy changes, the world you live in begins to change as well.

So what do spells do for you? First of all, spells align your energetic vibration with your personal goals and desires. Second, spells put your intentions and desires out into the universe, allowing the universe to help guide you. Third, spells allow you to let go so that your conscious mind doesn't interfere with how your intentions are manifested.

## How to Cast Spells

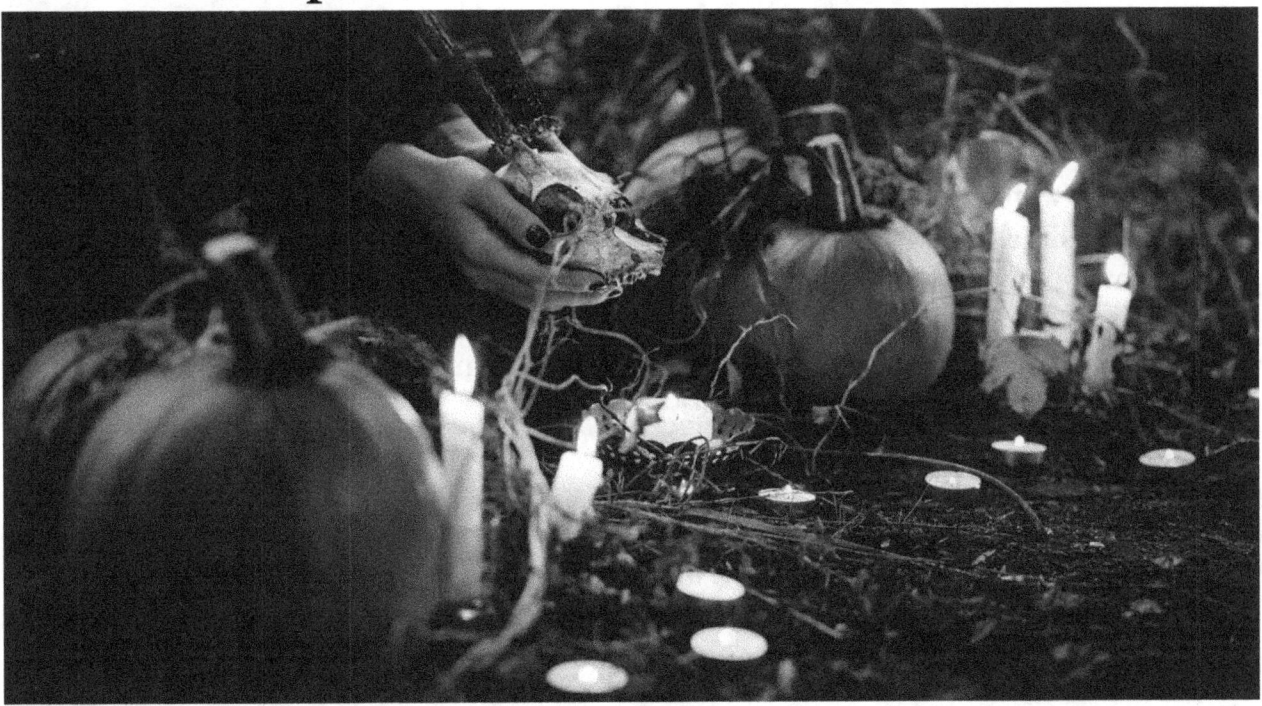

The actual act of casting a spell does generally require some ceremony. Not all spells have to be cast at your altar; however, this is going to be the main base for your casting.

Before you even start your spell, make sure you have all your needed supplies and ingredients at your altar. Once you start casting, you don't want to have to run off and grab something you forgot! Also, keep your Book of Shadows close and your spellbook, if you are using one.

You'll want the four elements represented on your altar. Fire can be a lit candle; air can be burning incense. Water can be as simple as a glass of water, and the earth could be a rock or pebble. If you have a fixed altar, you can get more creative as desired with the representations on your altar.

For spellcasting, you will also want candles and some kind of physical representation of the Goddess and God or whatever deities you appeal to.

Before getting into the spellcasting, you are going to want to cast your Sacred Circle. This circle will serve as a barrier between you and outside energies. It will prevent any energies from encroaching on your spell that does not serve its purpose.

There are many ways to cast a Sacred Circle, and some are very simple, while others are more complex.

A basic circle casting involves setting your altar at the center of your intended circle, then placing your rock or pebble at the north corner, your glass of water at the west corner, your lit candle at the south corner, and the burning incense at the east corner.

Holding your wand, start facing east and invoke air while standing in the east. Then walk in a deosil (clockwise) circle to the candle to invoke fire, then water in the west, and the earth in the north. Complete your circle back in the east.

Alternatively, you can stand at the center of your circle and face each direction, starting in the east and turning deosil (clockwise).

Basic elemental invocations can sound like:

> *Here do I call in Air at the East, to fill my circle with the breath of life*
>
> *Here do I call in Fire at the South, to fill my circle with warmth and strength*
>
> *Here do I call in Water at the West, to cleanse my circle and fill it with life*
>
> *Here do I call in Earth at the North, to create a strong foundation for my circle*

Step to the center of your circle and stand at your altar to invoke the deity. You can continue to hold your wand or set it down.

An invocation for deity could sound like:

> *Mother Goddess and Father God, I invite that you join my circle, that you guard and guide me during this spell*

Once the invocations are made, you can complete the circle by saying:

> *I create sacred space, so mote it be*

Now that your circle has been cast, it is time to start preparing your spell. Sit in front of your altar and first close your eyes and take a few long, deep breaths. At this point, you should state your intention and visualize the goal of your spell.

Once you have a clear picture in your mind, begin to move through the designated tasks and actions of your spell. Keep your visualization strong during these actions and tasks to enhance the spell's power further.

The next step is to raise magical power and energy for your spell. This can be done through focused imagination and visualization. Really see your goal coming true and envision it as if the spell has already worked its magic.

Other methods of raising power include:

- Dancing
- Chanting
- Singing
- Incantation
- Playing an instrument (drum, rattle, flute, recorder, etc.)

As you raise the power, feel the magic stirring within you and around you. The power comes from within, but it also comes from the world and the universe. As power is raised, you'll be able to feel it. Sometimes, it takes practice and time for you to feel magic, but keep yourself open to magic and power.

After you have raised and focused your power, you may find yourself needing to ground yourself again. That energy can fill you up and make you feel a little dizzy or light-headed.

To ground yourself, sit cross-legged, and put your hands on the floor or ground. If you are outside, touch a rock or a tree. If you have crystals, rock salt, or tree bark inside, hold or touch something earthy to help yourself connect back to your body.

Once you have released your power, your spell will begin to work. You can continue to stay in your circle and meditate or close your Sacred Circle.

When closing your circle, thank the deity and elements. You can thank them individually or all at once. An example of a thanking incantation can sound like:

> *Thank you, Goddess, God, and the four elements for joining in my Circle. This circle is undone but not broken. Merry did we come here, merry do we part, to merry come again.*

You'll want to extinguish your candles and clean up your space after.

When casting spells, if you make a charm or use an amulet or talisman, most spells will indicate whether you are supposed to bury the object, carry it on your person for any amount of time, keep it under your pillow, or hang in a specific space.

Since the magic continues to work after the spell is cast, it is important to follow these instructions to enhance the success of the spell.

Additionally, continue to visualize and take steps to accomplish your goals. Your spell will need continued participation from you to keep the magic working.

Spellcasting isn't limited to just your altar or sacred space that you have designated for practicing Wicca. Spells can be cast pretty much anywhere, as long as you have the tools and supplies you want or need for a given spell.

If you are casting a spell in a location other than at your altar, you should still be invoking a deity, the four directions, and setting an intention for a safe space. While you don't necessarily need a full Sacred Circle, holding a safe and protected space for yourself will prevent outside energies from influencing your spell.

A simple space holding intention can sound like:

> *I intend that this (room, car, space, etc.) becomes a safe and sacred space for my spellcasting.*

Types of spells that may need to be cast in a designated location away from your altar include:

- Room cleansing
- Home protection
- Weather dances
- Fire rituals (should be performed around a safe fireplace or woodstove if inside or around a closed fire pit outside. Always adhere to local fire laws and safety.)
- Car protection

Depending on the kinds of spells that you find yourself casting, having a mini or portable altar is another option if you do not want a fixed location for your altar. Some Wiccans will keep an altar inside their house and a separate altar outside their house for outdoor rituals and spells.

Spellcasting can be creative and subjective. When you first start, you will probably be looking for prewritten spells to try. This book has plenty of those! However, you may find that you want to start writing your own spells, too.

## Spellcrafting

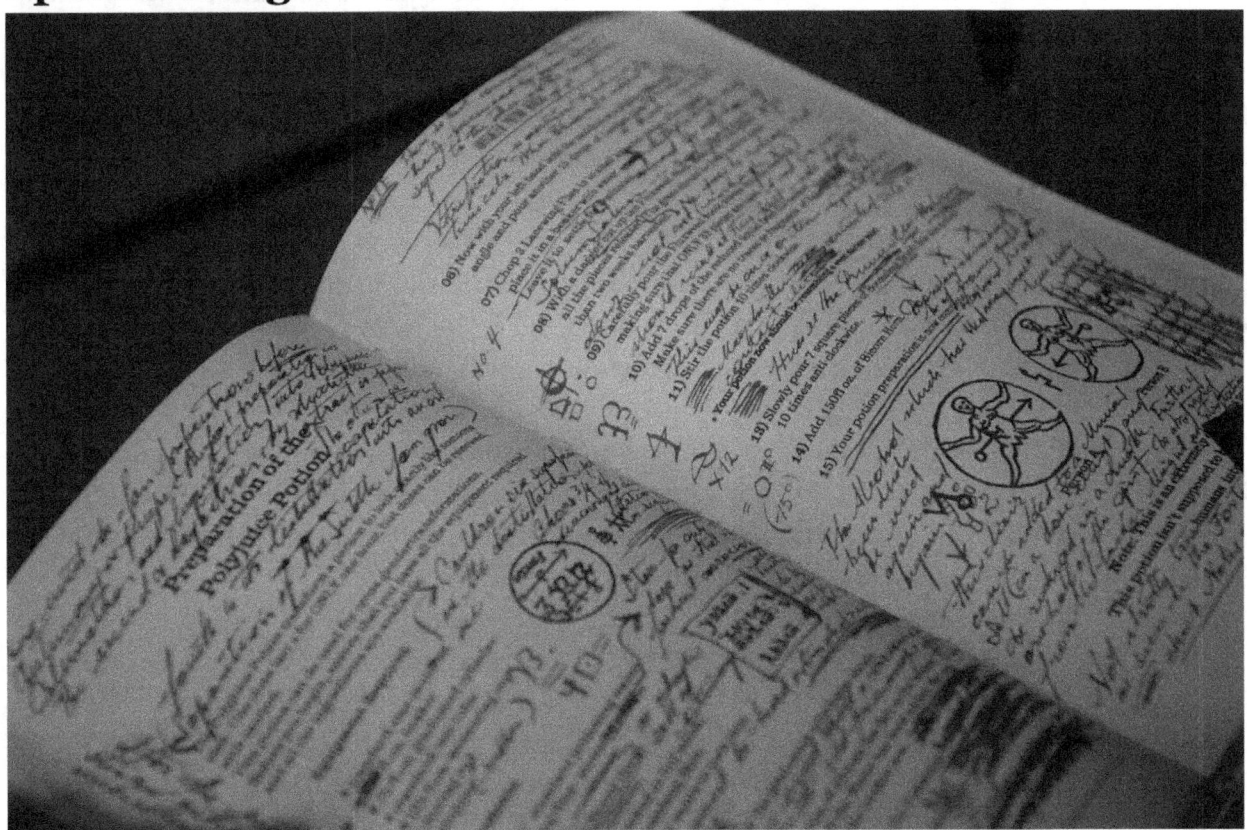

Spellcrafting is the art of writing and designing your own spells. While it is recommended that you start out with prewritten spells, many Wiccans enjoy making their own.

Why write your own spells if so many are readily available? Sometimes Wiccans write spells out of necessity if they haven't found the specific kind of spell they want to cast. Sometimes, Wiccans will write spells or adapt spells based on what ingredients and tools are available to them. Then some Wiccans just prefer to create their own spells for a personal flare, just as they prefer making their own tools for the craft.

Adding your own personal power to spells by writing them is going to help them align with your energy. Spells aligned with your personal energy are more effective for your goals.

Writing spells is a little bit of a learned skill. This is primarily because of all the different variable sin spells. Magic comes from so many forms, candles, colors, herbs, chanting, crystals, etc. Understanding the magical and medicinal properties of the ingredients that go into spells is going to be necessary for writing your own spells.

For example, if you are writing a spell for love, you'll want to include ingredients and tools that resonate with the feeling of love, such as a Rose Quartz, or pink flower petals, or a red candle.

Having a basic knowledge and understanding of common spell ingredients is recommended if you are interested in writing your own spells.

The good news is that spells don't have to be masterfully written or composed as poetry. Many incantations rhyme or have a flowing pattern to them, but that isn't necessary. Generally, spells written as couplets or in rhyme tend to be easier to remember. If you are writing your spells down, then you can always refer back to them.

To write a spell, you will first need to know your intention or goal. It is a good idea to start with a piece of paper and write your intention, then let the ingredients, incantation, and spell actions unfold. Once you have everything together, you can write it out as formally or informally as you'd like in your Book of Shadows.

Let's say you want to attract money. At the top of your paper, write 'Attract Money.'

Next, list some colors and ingredients that go along with money and wealth. Write them down, in this case, 'Green, patchouli, basil, and sage.'

This is going to be a very simple money spell, so the two spell ingredients are going to be a green candle and patchouli essential oil.

Now we should write our incantation. You might need to throw some words down, and see what starts to sound right or what resonates with you. This specific money incantation will look like:

> *Bring more money to me*
> *This is my will, so mote it be*
> *With these words, this spell I cast*

*I will this magic to act fast*

The words don't have to be complicated or scholarly. As long as the incantation meets your intention, and you continue to visualize your goal, the spell will act accordingly.

Now that you have the intention, ingredients, and incantation, how do you put it all together?

The actions of the spell are simple. Remember, when working with candles, you want to cleanse it first. Then you'll want to anoint your candle with the Patchouli oil. Anointing is also when you will say your incantation for the first time.

To anoint your candle, put a drop of patchouli oil on your forefinger; starting at the top of your candle, anoint down until you reach the middle of the candle. Put another drop of oil on your forefinger and start from the bottom of the candle, anointing up until you reach the middle of your candle. The two streaks of oil will meet in the middle.

This is the anointing method for spells you are using to attract something to you; in this case, money.

Once the candle is anointed, set it on your altar and light the candle. Say your incantation three times willfully and strongly, visualizing your goal and then extinguish the candle. Repeat the burning and incanting steps for three consecutive nights and then bury the remaining candle stub outside.

Now, when you go to actually write your spell down in a Book of Shadows or Grimoire, it might end up looking more like this.

## Spell to Attract Money

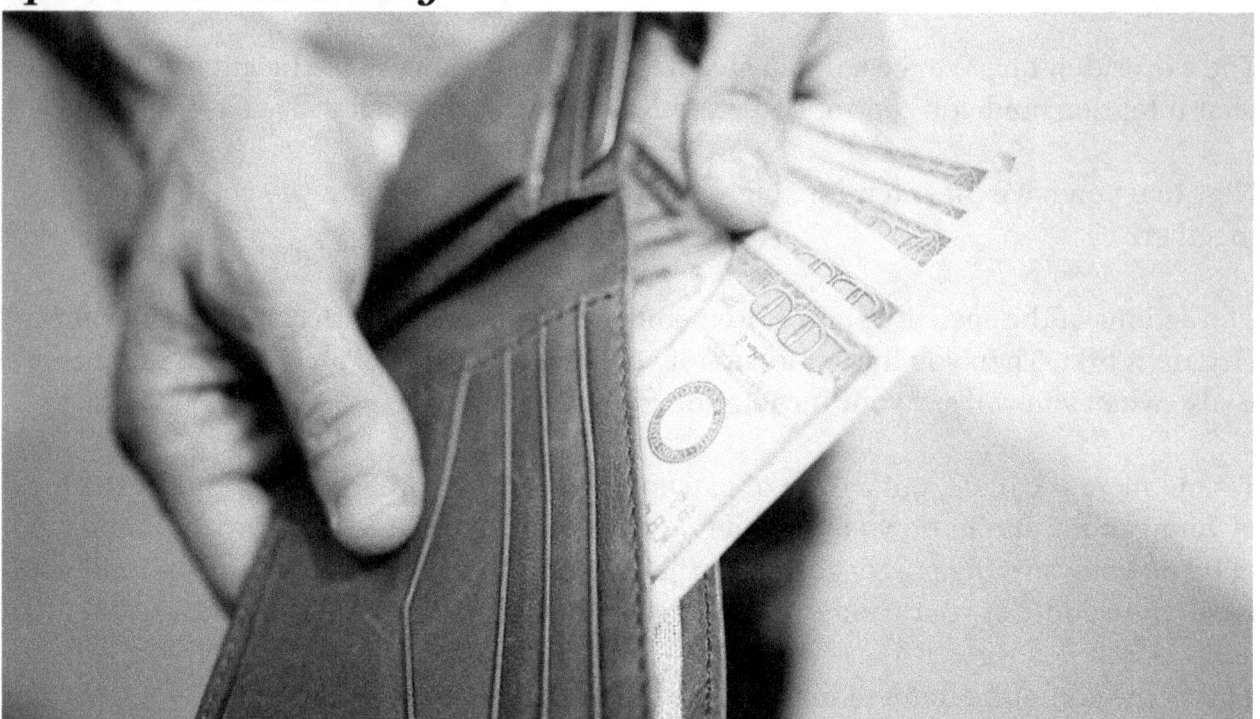

Supplies:
    Green candle
    Patchouli oil

Instructions:
- Open/Cast Sacred Circle
- Cleanse green candle
- Anoint the candle with patchouli oil while visualizing your goal, and say this incantation:

*Bring more money to me*
*This is my will, so mote it be*
*With these words, this spell I cast*
*I will this magic to act fast*

- Set your candle on the altar and light the candle.
- Repeat the incantation three times.
- Extinguish the candle.
- Close the circle.
- Repeat the burning and incanting steps for three consecutive nights.
- Bury the remaining candle stub outside.

- Continue to visualize your goal after your spell is cast.

You may notice that a lot of spells call for papers to be folded in thirds or incantations repeated three times. Three is a powerful magical number and is used frequently in spells to enhance their power.

However, you will find it easiest to write your spells out so that you can refer back to them and know that what they mean is fine. Writing spells can be fun and empowering, and they get you to think creatively about your Wiccan lifestyle. Even if you don't think you'll be interested, you are encouraged to at least give it a try.

# Chapter Four: Spells for Friendship

As you start to work with spells and begin to cast, and possibly write your own spell, you will begin to see how varied the spells and their ingredients can be. Just because a spell is simple, it doesn't mean that it is less effective. The power comes from you and your intention!

Spells that deal with friendship encompass several subcategories of sorts. In this chapter, you will discover spells for attracting new friends. There will be spells to help friends, strengthen friendships, peacefully end friendships, find an animal companion or familiar, resolve conflict with friends, and other similar topics.

If any of the spells cover working on a specific friend, such as helping a friend pass a test or helping them find their lost wallet, remember that you should have their expressed permission before casting the spell.

Friends can come in many forms. Sometimes, they are people, animals, or even natural objects, such as trees or rocks. Humans are social animals, and loneliness is a terrible feeling. It can be hard to connect with other people. Friendships change as people grow and move and change. Sometimes, friends pass away or move away, and this can leave a void.

There are many emotions and circumstances that involve friends. The spells in this chapter are going to touch on several situations that can be encountered with existing friends or in the pursuit of new friends.

Sometimes, spells are stronger when cast by two Wiccans. Included in the spells below are a few friendship spells designed to be cast with a friend, ideally, another practicing Wiccan.

## *Blessing a Friend*

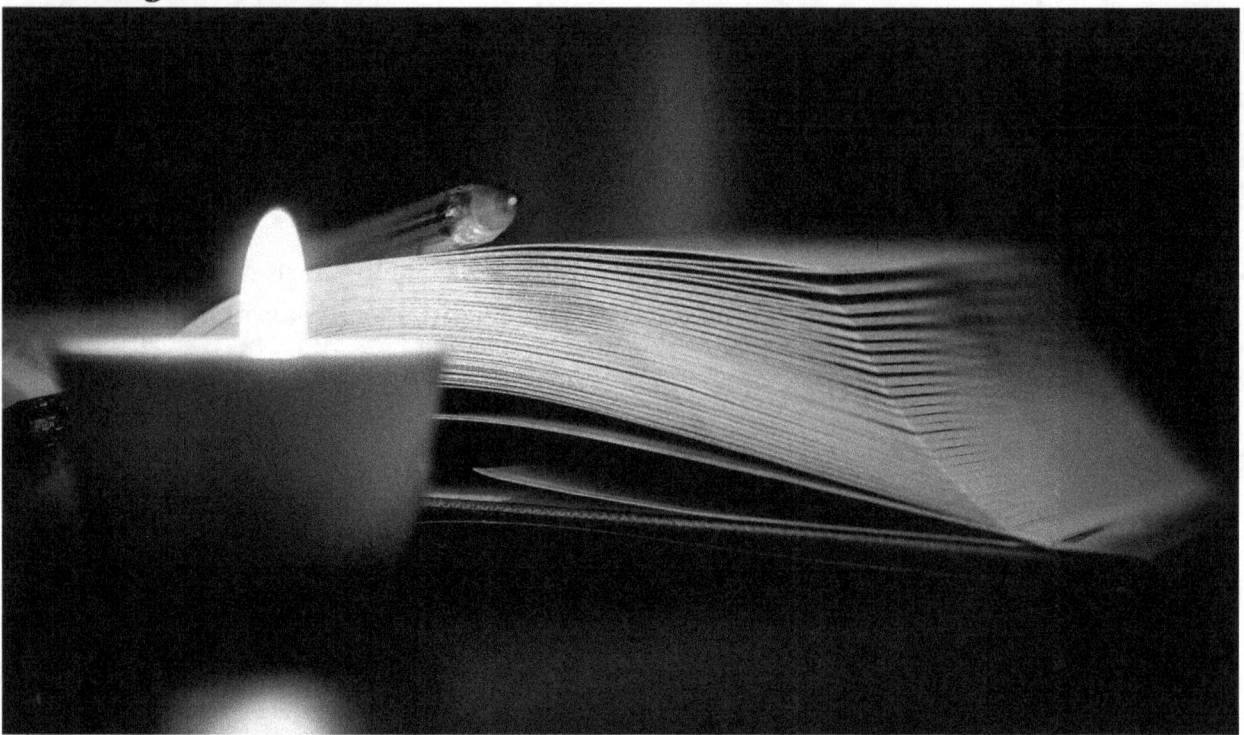

Cast this spell at the Full Moon to bless a friend.

    Supplies:
        White Candle
        Blessed or Holy Oil
        Paper and Pen or Personal Item of Friend

Instructions:
- Get friend's permission to cast this spell, and use a personal item of theirs in the spell.
- Cast a Sacred Circle.
- Cleanse the white candle
- Carve friend's name or personal symbols on the wax of the candle.
- Anoint the candle with blessing oil.
- Set the candle on the altar, on top of a piece of paper with their name or beside a personal item that belongs to this friend.
- Burn a portion of the candle every day for 7 consecutive days.
- While the candle is burning, say this incantation:
  > *[Friend's Name] you are blessed. May good things come to you and may you be free of negativity and harm. Your heart is full of*

*light. May your journeys be safe, may you remain healthy, and may your mind stay strong. You are blessed.*
- Close the Circle.
- After seven days, bury the remaining candle stub.
- Write down the incantation for your friend to keep if they wish.

## *Attracting a New Friend*

Cast this spell during the Waxing Moon to attract new friends to you.

>Supplies:
>>Three brown candles
>>Blank paper and pen
>>Heatproof dish

Instructions:
- Open the Sacred Circle.
- Light three brown candles on your altar.
- On the blank paper, write down a list of attributes you'd like in a friend. Be as detailed as possible. Include personality traits, physical features, and any historical or background information you want them to have or relate to. Visualize them clearly as they are written and spoken.
- As you write your list, speak each item aloud.
- Fold your paper three times.
- Light the edge on one of the candle flames.
- Put the burning paper in your heatproof dish.
- While the paper burns, say this incantation:
  > *With heart and mind, I speak*
  > *Draw to me the one I seek*
  > *Let this list be their guide*
  > *To bring this friend to my side*
  > *Pain and loneliness will be no more*
  > *Bring an ally to my door*
  > *With pleasures great and sorrows few*
  > *We shall build this friendship new*
  > *With my words, this spell is done*
  > *Do as ye will and harm ye none*
- Let the paper burn out.
- Close the circle.
- Scatter the ash to the wind.
- Continue to visualize and imagine the friend that you seek entering your life.

## *Hearing From a Friend You Miss*

Cast this spell during a Waxing Moon to encourage communication from a friend that you miss and have not heard from recently.

    Supplies:
        Blank paper
        Black pen
        White candle
        Heatproof dish

Instructions:
- Open a circle.
- Cleanse the white candle and then light it on your altar.
- By candlelight, write a letter to a friend that you miss or have not heard from in a while. As you write the letter, visualize how you would feel when they contacted you. Think of how you miss them, and try to remember the last time you saw them in person or the last time you spoke to them.
- When your letter is written, fold it in half three times.
- Say this incantation three times:
    *From you, I wish to hear*
    *You may be far, but I feel you near*
    *Do harm to none*
    *This spell is done*

- Light the letter on the white candle, and let burn in a heatproof dish to release it into the universe, or send the letter to your friend for a more direct approach.
- Close the circle.

## *Friendship Knot*

Cast this spell as a charm to draw a new friend into your life. It is best to cast during a Waxing Moon.

Supplies:
- White string, 12 inches
- Gray string, 12 inches
- Pink string, 12 inches
- Blank paper and pen

Instructions:
- Cast a sacred circle.
- Take a moment to meditate on why you are seeking a new friend. Write the reason down on your blank paper. This part is important as understanding your desire for a new friend can better help you connect with the right kind of friend you currently need.
- Next, write a list of the 12 most important traits you would like your new friend to have. Speak the traits aloud and clearly visualize them.
- Hold your three strings together, and for each trait, tie a knot in the strings. Space them about 1 inch apart.
- As you tie a knot, speak aloud the trait that it represents.
- Close the circle.
- Wear your charm as a bracelet or necklace, or tie it to your keychain or purse.
- Periodically touch your charm and visualize the chosen traits again.
- Keep it on your person until a new friend enters your life.

## Dream Pet Spell

Cast this spell during the Waxing Moon to attract an animal companion to you.

    Supplies:
        Small container with lid (jar, bottle, etc.)
        Water
        Blank paper and pen
        Artistic tools (optional)
        Object representing animal you want

Instructions:
- Open a Sacred Circle.
- On a blank paper, draw the type of pet you want. Be as detailed and artistic as you want, adding color and minor details if you like. (Please keep in mind that magic has limits; stick to animals that are known to exist, and try to keep to pets that are legal or can be easily acquired in your geographical region).
- Underneath your drawing, list characteristics you would like your pet to have. Include physical traits, personality traits, and any quirks or special traits you want them to have.
- Strongly visualize your animal companion and speak the traits aloud.
- Fold the paper three times and say this incantation three times:

> *An animal companion I desire*
> *This pet, please help me acquire*
> *Let us form a lasting trust*
> *Harm none is a must*

- Fill the container up with water, leaving a little room at the top
- Add an object that relates to your desired pet (a ball for a dog, milk for a cat, grass for a horse, a branch for a bird, etc.).
- Finally, place the folded paper in the container of water with the animal object
- Close the lid on the container.
- Close your circle.
- Set the container somewhere you think your pet would enjoy. Give the water time to dissolve the paper and continue to visualize your ideal animal companion.

## *Repair a Friendship*

Cast this spell during the Waxing Moon to help repair a friendship. Whether you've had a fight, disagreement, or falling out, this spell will help you to reach a resolution.

Supplies:
- Pink candle
- Blank paper and pen
- Envelope
- Material to make a gift for your friend

Instructions:
- Open the Sacred Circle.
- Cleanse the pink candle.
- Carve a symbol for friendship on the wax of the pink candle.
- Carve additional symbols for peace or love on the candle if you wish.
- Light the candle and meditate for a few moments on the disagreement that you had with your friend.
- Visualize a mended friendship, and say this incantation:
    *Two friends have had a fight*
    *Please help to set this right*
    *Help us to remain friends*
    *Let us make amends*
- At the top of the blank paper, draw the symbols you carved into the candle. Then begin to write down your feelings about repairing the friendship. If there is anything you would like to apologize for or accept responsibility for, write that down. Write down what you would like to happen with this friendship, as well as the reasons you want to remain friends.
- Sign your name on the paper.
- Make a small yet thoughtful gift for your friend.
- While making the gift, continue to visualize a mended friendship and your overall desires for this spell.
- Put the gift and the paper inside the envelope and seal the envelope with wax from the pink candle.
- Close the circle.
- When you next see your friend, give them the envelope.

## *Spell for Everlasting Friendship*

At the Full Moon, cast this spell with a friend you wish to keep in your life forever.

> Supplies:
> 2 glass jars or bottles with lids
> Dried Apple Blossom petals
> Dried Pink Rose petals
> White sugar
> White Candle
> Red Candle

Instructions:
- Open the Sacred Circle.
- Cleanse the white and red candles.
- Light the candles on your altar.
- Stand with your friend before the altar, and take a jar or bottle each.
- Fill the jars with a combination of the flower petals, and top off with a handful of white sugar.
- While filling your jars, imagine the jar filled with love, friendship, and longevity. Visualize a strong, lasting friendship and how it will look when you are still friends years and years from now. Add trust, forgiveness, loyalty, and kindness for your friend into the jar.

- Put the lids on the jars and say this incantation together:
    *Most friendships come and grow*
    *Please allow ours to always grow*
    *By our will, so mote it be*
    *Friends forever, times three*
- After the incantation, exchange friendship jars with each other.
- Blow out the candles.
- Close the circle.
- Keep your respective jars in your bedrooms or personal space.

## *Protection for a Friend*

Cast this spell at the Full or Waning Moon to provide a friend with protection.

> Supplies:
> > Picture of friend or personal object
> > White candle
> > Light blue candle

Instructions:
- Get a friend's expressed permission before casting a spell on their behalf.
- Cast a Sacred Circle.
- Cleanse white and light blue candles
- Light candles and set image of a friend or personal object in between the two candles.
- Visualize a strong protective barrier around your friend.
- Make sure it is a barrier for protection against physical harm and psychic harm.
- Say this incantation three times while holding the protective barrier visualization:
  > *Protection for (friend's name) is my desire*
  > *Please grant them strength and courage of fire*
  > *Keep them safe from harm to body and mind*
  > *This protection spell I bind*
  > *Do harm to none*
  > *This spell is done*
- Re-visualize that protective barrier for your friend.
- Blow out the candles.
- Close the circle.
- Burn the candles and repeat incanting for three consecutive nights.
- Bury the remaining candle stubs outside.

## Finding Forgiveness

During the Waning Moon, cast this spell to receive forgiveness from a friend.

    Supplies:
        White candle
        Lavender incense

Instructions:
- Open the Sacred Circle.
- Cleanse the white candle.
- On the altar, light the white candle and the lavender incense.
- Meditate, deeply breathing in the scent and smoke of the incense.
- Visualize yourself receiving forgiveness and being forgiven.
- Repeat this incantation three times:
    *To err is human*
    *To forgive is transcendent*
    *Please grant me forgiveness*
    *I seek release and independence*
- Return to a meditative state while visualizing yourself receiving forgiveness and being forgiven .
- Blow out the candle.

- Close the circle.
- Repeat the candle burning, meditation, and incanting for seven consecutive days.

## *Peacefully End a Friendship*

During the Waning Moon, cast this spell to amicably break a friendship bond that no longer serves you.

Supplies:
An object that represents the friendship (friendship bracelet; a gift from them)
A bowl of dirt or sand

Instructions:
- Open the Sacred Circle.
- On the altar, bury the friendship object in the bowl of dirt or sand. Completely cover the item, so it can't be seen at all.
- Repeat this incantation at least three times, more if your intuition tells you to:
    *Tonight, I banish this toxic bond*
    *Under the waning moon and beyond*
    *Let us both retreat on peaceful terms*
    *Harm none, this I confirm*
- Visualize the friendship ending on amicable terms. Think of your friend and why they no longer fit into your life. Give a silent thanks for their friendship and wish them well without you in their life.
- Close the circle.
- Repeat incantation over a burred object as frequently as you feel the need.
- Once the friendship is ended, bury the dirt or sand and the friendship object outside far away from home, work, or school.

# Friendship Potion (Drinkable)

During the days of the Waxing Moon, prepare and cast this spell to attract new friendships.

    Supplies:
- Drink pitcher
- Water
- Strawberries
- Lemon Juice
- Fresh Mint Leaves

Instructions:
- A day before you want to cast the spell cut the strawberries. Fill the pitcher with cold water and then add the strawberries. Keep it in the refrigerator overnight.
- Cast your sacred circle.
- Take 1 cup of the strawberry water in a cup.
- Add one drop of lemon juice to the strawberry water at the beginning of each line of the incantation.
- Say this incantation:
    *Earth, water, fire, air*
    *Send to me a friend who cares*
    *Please bring me a kindred soul*

> *Two halves make a friendship whole*
> *Through good and bad a friendship keeps*
> *This is my will, so mote it be*

- Stir the strawberry water and lemon juice together. Stir in a clockwise direction
- Garnish the drink with fresh mint.
- Drink your drink and visualize a new friend entering your life.
- Drink slowly and imagine all the details and qualities that you want in a new friend.
- When the glass is empty, spend a few moments meditating on your new friend at your altar.
- Close the circle.
- Repeat spell with remaining strawberry water one cup at a time.

## *Find an Animal Totem or Guide*

Cast this spell on a Full Moon night to find your animal guide. Cast this spell just before you go to sleep.

>Supplies:
>>Book of Shadows or Grimoire
>>Pen
>>White candle

Instructions:
- Cast your Sacred Circle.
- Cleanse the white candle.
- Light the candle on your altar and open your Grimoire or Book of Shadows to a blank page for a journal entry.
- Write this incantation in your Grimoire or Book of Shadows:
    > *Guardians of my dreams, open mine eyes wide*
    > *Lead me to my spirit protector and guide*
    > *Show me the magical path to walk*
    > *So that we may communicate and talk*
- Meditate on that incantation while the white candle burns low. Visualize yourself finding your animal totem and guide.
- Blow out the candle.
- Close your circle.
- Sleep with your Book of Shadows next to your bed, and write down any details from dreams you have as soon as you wake up.
- Your dreams will guide you to your spirit animal. Spirit animals can be very useful on your Wiccan path.

## Strengthen a Friendship

Cast this spell on the Full Moon to strengthen the bond you have with a friend.

Supplies:
- Brown Candle
- Yellow paper
- Pen
- Heatproof container

Instructions:
- Open your Sacred Circle.
- Cleanse the candle.
- Carve symbols of friendship into the candle and light it on your altar.
- Draw your friendship symbols on the yellow paper. Write words you associate with friendship and words you associate with the friend whom you are looking to strengthen the relationship with.
- Visualize the two of you growing closer together and forming a stronger friendship bond.
- Fold the yellow paper three times and write, 'Harm None' on the outside of the paper.

- Light the yellow paper from the brown candle flame.
- Transfer the paper to the heatproof dish and allow to burn.
- Keep visualizing your strengthened friendship bond until the paper burns out.
- Close the circle.
- Disperse paper ash into the wind.

## *Finding a True Friend*

During the Waxing Moon, cast this spell to find a true, loyal, lifelong friend.

    Supplies:
        Pink candle
        Candle of your favorite color
        Sandalwood essential oil
        Pink string
        String of your favorite color

Instructions:
- Open your Sacred Circle.
- Cleanse both candles.
- Anoint the candle that is your favorite color with sandalwood oil and say:
  *With all my individuality*
  *This candle now represents me*
- Anoint the pink candle with the sandalwood oil and say:
  *With all their individuality*
  *This candle now represents a friend's personality*
- Light both candles on your altar and say this incantation:
  *I draw a friend to me, loyal and true*
  *By the loving power of two*
  *Our bond will grow strong and tight*
  *By both our wills, sealed by candlelight*
- Blow both candles out.
- Use the two colored strings to tie the candles together, visualizing a new friend coming into your life. Visualize details in personality or appearance that you want this friend to have.
- Close the circle.
- Leave the bound candles on your altar until a new friend enters your life.

## *Friendship Bag*

This charm is best to cast during a Waxing Moon to help attract new friends.

    Supplies:
        Orange or yellow natural fiber fabric
        White or yellow string
        Yellow or Red rose petals
        Penny
        Red or yellow crystal or stone

Instructions:
- Open your Sacred Circle.
- Lay the fabric open on your altar; square or circular cut is the easiest shape to work with.
- Put the rose petals in the center of the fabric.
- Hold the crystal or stone in your dominant hand and say this incantation three times:

    *Bring to me new friends true*
    *Bind us together like with glue*
    *Let our friendship grow strong*
    *Find us a place to belong*

- Set the crystal into the bag, and pick up the penny with your dominant hand.
- Visualize the kinds of friends you want to make, including details for their personalities and even physical appearances. Envision what it will be like to have these friends.
- Kiss the penny for good luck, and add it to the bag.
- Fold the edges of the fabric, and use the colored string to tie the fabric around the ingredients and into a bag.
- Close your circle.
- Carry your charm bag on your person or in a bag.
- Periodically touch the charm bag and give it a squeeze, releasing the magic and visualizing your intended goal.

The spells in this chapter are designed to be an introduction to spellcasting and give you a starting point to play around with spells. Any spells that are pre-written can be altered and adapted as needed for your uses.

Friendships can be complicated, emotional, hard to start, and hard to keep. They can also be enjoyable, everlasting, and strong support systems. In any situation, remember to feel grateful for the solid, good friendships you have and try to remove yourself from toxic friendships.

You can find friends in people, family members, animals, spirits, and other entities. Even a spirit guide or animal totem can become a friend, confidant, and support system as you walk the Wiccan path.

www.ingramcontent.com/pod-product-compliance
Lightning Source LLC
Chambersburg PA
CBHW081754100526
44592CB00015B/2439